# THE ULTIMATE GUIDE TO HEALING CODEPENDENCY

*Breaking Free From People-Pleasing,*
*And Being Overly Involved*

**Brian White**

# COPYRIGHT PAGE

# INTRODUCTION

There is a phenomenon that subtly permeates the lives of many people, affecting their emotional landscapes and behavioural patterns in the complex web of human interactions.

Co-dependency is the name of these phenomena, which is often cryptic and hidden behind the nuances of relationship.

This is "The Ultimate Guide to Healing Co-dependency: Breaking Free from People-Pleasing and Being Overly Involved." This thorough investigation seeks to clarify the complexities of co-dependency and provides a transforming path to recovery and self-discovery.

The study of relationships including drug usage served as the original inspiration for the word co-dependency, which has since grown in meaning and application.

Since then, however, it has broadened to include a wider variety of situations in which a person's identity and sense of self-worth are strongly influenced by the wants, desires, and acceptance of others.

It may take many different forms: it might be an overt fixation with running someone else's life or it can be a subtly surrendering of personal boundaries. The goal of this book is to analyse these expressions in order to shed light on an illness that has far too long been stigmatized and shrouded in mystery.

It is not an easy road to understanding co-dependency and recovering from it. It is loaded with the nuanced aspects of our personalities, the complicated dance of our relationships, and the complexity of our pasts.

Confronting the often unpleasant facts of our habits and the causes underlying them demands fortitude. In addition to providing that insight, this book lays out doable, practical measures for healing and development.

You will be prompted to consider, question, and eventually alter the patterns that have imprisoned you as you read through the pages of this book.

You may wonder why this trip is required. Unchecked co-dependency has a heavy price tag that impacts not just the person but also everyone around them.

When the emotional work is divided unevenly in relationships, it may result in imbalanced and unhealthy partnerships that often cause resentment, conflict, and fatigue.

Co-dependency may permeate social interactions, one's career, and even one's relationship with oneself, beyond the boundaries of intimate relationships. This can result in a persistent feeling of discontent and detachment.

Thus, ending the cycle of co-dependency is a liberating act as well as a means of self-preservation. It's about taking back your independence, your identity, and your capacity for fulfilling, respectful, and reciprocal relationships.

This book will walk you through the process of comprehending the causes of co-dependent behaviours, which are often derived from upbringing, cultural standards, and society expectations.

It will examine the emotional and psychological underpinnings of these habits and provide guidance on how to start breaking them down.

The power of consciousness is one of this guide's main principles. The first step towards transformation is awareness. We might begin to see the potential for something else as we become more aware of the patterns that characterize co-dependency.

This book offers techniques and methods to increase this awareness, such as case studies, introspective activities, and useful guidance for overcoming obstacles on the road to recovery.

Furthermore, you are not required to go alone on this adventure. The handbook places a strong emphasis on the value of assistance, whether it comes from friends, family, counselling, or support groups.

Others' empathy, understanding, and support are crucial throughout the process of recovering from co-dependency. It's a process that is fundamentally social and yet quite intimate.

We will examine the several aspects of co-dependency in the next chapters, including how it affects boundaries and self-worth, how it shows itself in relationships, and how it affects mental and emotional health.

We'll examine methods for creating more positive bonds with others and, most crucially, with oneself. This book focuses on leading a life that is more real, joyful, and free of co-dependency rather than merely helping readers escape it.

You are making a significant step toward recovery and change by starting this journey.

More than simply a book, "The Ultimate Guide to Healing Co-dependency: Breaking Free From People-Pleasing and Being Overly Involved" is a journey partner that will help you become a happier, healthier version of yourself.

Let's investigate the depths of co-dependency together in order to open the door to a life free from the weight of seeking approval from others and filled with the beauty of real connection.

# CHAPTER 1

# WHAT IS CO-DEPENDENCY?

A complex psychological idea, co-dependency affects both our self-perception and our interpersonal interactions. Co-dependency is essentially a behavioural pattern in which people become overly dependent on other people to meet their emotional and psychological requirements.

It frequently results from trauma, early events, or dysfunctional family dynamics that alter an individual's perspective on relationships. A more thorough investigation of co-dependency's causes is necessary to comprehend it.

People who suffer from co-dependency frequently come from homes where boundaries were blurred and emotions were repressed. People who grow up in such an atmosphere may not develop emotionally healthily and instead turn to other people for approval and a sense of value.

Co-dependency is fundamentally a warped sense of self in which an individual's identity is entwined with that of others. People may put the needs of others before their own, compromising their well-being to keep connections intact.

This behaviour frequently leads to an endless loop of

looking to other people for validation and acceptance, which erodes one's feeling of self-worth.

Moreover, co-dependency can show up in a variety of ways, including encouraging harmful conduct in others, going above and above to please others, and having a persistent dread of being rejected or abandoned.

People get so driven by their incessant need for approval from others that they lose sight of their own needs and wants. Acknowledging one's co-dependency is an essential first step toward recovery.

It entails introspection and a sincere assessment of one's actions and motives in interpersonal interactions. People may see behavioural patterns in which they unconsciously put the needs of others above their happiness and well-being.

It takes a journey of self-discovery and the establishment of healthier relationship dynamics to overcome co-dependency. It entails developing self-acceptance and self-love, as well as learning to set limits and encourage independence.

In order to prepare readers for the transforming journey that awaits them in the upcoming chapters, this chapter attempts to provide them with a basic grasp of co-dependency.

Co-dependency is the result of a complicated interaction between emotional and psychological elements that affect how people react to one another and to themselves.

Starting the journey to escaping this pattern and creating happier, healthier relationships requires identifying the symptoms and comprehending the causes of co-dependency.

# CHAPTER 2
# SIGNS OF CODEPENDENCY

For those who want to escape the complex web of toxic relationship dynamics, identifying the symptoms of co-dependency is essential.

To shed light on the complications people may encounter in their interpersonal relationships, we will go deeper into the observable behavioural and emotional patterns that indicate co-dependency in this chapter.

The intense need to win people over is one of the main signs of co-dependency. This widespread tendency to please others is frequently the result of a deep-seated yearning for approval from others.

Co-dependency traps people into going above and beyond to satisfy the demands and expectations of people around them, frequently at the price of their own wellbeing.

When one's continual quest for acceptance takes precedence over admitting and satisfying one's own needs and preferences, this pattern can cause a progressive loss of one's sense of self.

The intense fear of being rejected or abandoned is a similarly related indication. People who are co-dependent frequently have a great fear of disagreement or conflict.

This dread often stems from earlier experiences where voicing one's wants or ideas were met with bad outcomes, such as childhood trauma or dysfunctional family dynamics.

As such, co-dependents may repress their own needs to preserve peace, unintentionally extending the cycle of reliance.

Additionally, an over-reliance on outside approval for one's own worth is a common sign of co-dependency. People in co-dependent relationships could get stuck in a cycle where their worth depends on other people's acceptance and approval.

People may experience a brittle and unstable sense of self-worth as a result of this external locus of validation, which makes it difficult for them to develop a true and stable sense of self-worth apart from outside validation.

Moreover, a prevalent characteristic of co-dependency is the blurring of boundaries. Unhealthy and entangled relationship dynamics can result from people's inability to distinguish their own wants and feelings from those of others.

Because co-dependent people may find it difficult to voice their own demands or make independent judgments, this lack of boundaries can impede personal growth and autonomy. Breaking out from the co-dependent cycle requires understanding and addressing these boundary issues.

It is crucial to stress that co-dependency is a spectrum condition as we work through these indicators. People may display different levels of these behaviours; the intention is not to categorize but to raise awareness, which acts as a trigger for constructive change.

People might start to unravel the complex web of co-dependency by identifying these symptoms. The impact of co-dependency and how these patterns affect emotional health and interpersonal relationships will be further explored in the upcoming chapters.

Equipped with this understanding, people can set out on a life-changing path, progressively releasing the bonds of co-dependency and cultivating relationships that are healthier and more harmonious.

# CHAPTER 3

# EFFECTS OF CODEPENDENCY

For individuals attempting to traverse the complex terrain of harmful relationship patterns, it is imperative to comprehend the profound repercussions of co-dependency.

This chapter seeks to explore the complex effects that co-dependency can have on people's mental, emotional, and even physical health. Co-dependency frequently results in bitterness and frustration on an emotional level.

Feeling neglected and unfulfilled might result from a never-ending cycle of putting other people's needs before of one's own. Emotional health slowly deteriorates as co-dependent people repress their own needs in order to live up to social norms.

The emotional toll of co-dependency is exacerbated by unmet demands and unexpressed emotions, which build up a reservoir of unhappiness. Co-dependency creates an atmosphere that is conducive to worry and low self-esteem, which has an equal negative effect on mental health.

One's self-worth is built on a shaky basis when they are always seeking approval from others. An ongoing concern about the stability of relationships might arise from a deep-seated fear of rejection or abandonment due to past experiences.

Co-dependency's porous boundaries can also make it difficult for a person to make independent decisions and confuse their sense of self, which can worsen mental suffering. Co-dependency's negative impacts might still affect one's physical health.

Chronic stress, which is frequently associated with co-dependent relationships, can cause physical symptoms like headaches, stomach problems, and sleep disruptions.

Prioritizing the needs of others over one's own can have a negative impact on one's health and have a domino effect on one's physical well-being.

Furthermore, co-dependent people unintentionally reinforce harmful habits by continuously putting the needs of the people they are in relationships with ahead of their own. This creates a loop of encouraging detrimental behaviours in others.

As individuals become involved in the repercussions of others' actions, this can exacerbate their sense of helplessness and increase the emotional strain that comes with co-dependency.

A comprehensive strategy that takes into account one's emotional, mental, and physical health is necessary to overcome the negative effects of co-dependency. Building healthier relationships and regaining one's sense of self begin with acknowledging the effects of co-dependency.

The techniques and resources for ending the co-dependency cycle will be discussed in the ensuing chapters, with an emphasis on developing emotional fortitude, a positive self-concept, and physical wellbeing.

People who are aware of the consequences of co-dependency can take a revolutionary step toward recovery, regaining emotional and mental balance, and creating a happier, healthier life.

# CHAPTER 4

# THE CYCLE OF CODEPENDENCY

For those who want to free themselves from the all-consuming grip of co-dependency, understanding the cycle of co-dependency is essential.

The complex processes that support and maintain co-dependency will be examined in detail in this chapter, illuminating the recurrent patterns that can be difficult to overcome.

A core need for acceptance and validation is frequently the starting point of the co-dependency cycle; motivated by the need to win over others, co-dependent people act in ways that put other people's ideas ahead of their own.

This first stage establishes the basis for the cycle, as the person's identity is deeply entwined with the expectations and wishes of individuals in their immediate vicinity.

As long as the co-dependent person puts other people before themselves, a pattern of supporting actions starts to show. This could entail continuously minimizing or ignoring the harmful deeds of others in an effort to preserve peace.

Through this process, co-dependent people unintentionally strengthen harmful behaviours, which further solidify the co-dependency cycle. At the same time, the cycle is maintained in large part by the dread of conflict and confrontation.

Co-dependent people keep their actual feelings and opinions to themselves out of fear of being rejected or abandoned. Because the surface seems peaceful and underlying issues fester unsolved, this avoidance breeds a false feeling of stability.

A cycle of repressed feelings and unfulfilled desires is sustained when issues are not addressed and discussed honestly. A lack of assertiveness when establishing limits feeds the cycle even more.

A persistent pattern of overextending oneself to please others might result from co-dependents finding it difficult to voice their own needs and boundaries.

The persistence of co-dependency is facilitated by this absence of boundaries, which creates an atmosphere in which other people's demands are constantly prioritized.

In addition, a deep fear of change feeds the cycle of co-dependency. A great deal of anxiety might be induced by the idea of claiming independence or going against established norms.

Because of the uncertainty and discomfort that come with change, co-dependent people may be resistant to ending the cycle. This apprehension about the unknown turns into a strong obstacle to starting the change required to escape the co-dependency cycle.

Disrupting these deeply rooted behaviours is essential to breaking free from the co-dependency cycle. In order to identify instances of enabling behaviour, conflict avoidance, and a lack of assertiveness, one must develop self-awareness.

To break the cycle, one must have the guts to voice their demands, establish firm limits, and accept the discomfort that comes with change. We shall examine doable tactics and methods to end the co-dependency cycle in the upcoming chapters.

People can start a path of self-discovery and empowerment and create relationships that are better and more balanced by knowing the factors that support this cycle.

# CHAPTER 5

# BREAKING THE CYCLE OF CODEPENDENCY

It takes a significant and life-changing effort to break the cycle of co-dependency, yet doing so is essential to building happier, healthier relationships.

This chapter seeks to provide a deeper exploration of the co-dependent cycle, shedding light on the recurring patterns that can trap people in toxic relationships.  The co-dependent cycle frequently begins with a strong focus on attending to other people's needs.

Many co-dependent people get their sense of identity and purpose from taking care of others and making things right in their relationships.  Even if it seems selfless, this outward focus becomes troublesome when it means putting one's own wants and desires last.

Though commendable, the innate need to provide for and encourage others can develop into a cycle in which the person's identity is absorbed into the caregiver position.

Co-dependents may find themselves more and more involved in the lives of those they look after as the cycle continues. Boundaries become hazy and one's sense of self is entangled with other people's happiness.

A progressive loss of personal autonomy may result from this entanglement, making it difficult for people to stand up for their own demands or make choices on their own. The co-dependent person unwittingly gives up their uniqueness in an effort to build relationships. The cycle's second stage introduces a subdued but ubiquitous sense of discontent.

A growing awareness of unmet personal needs exists despite ongoing efforts to meet the needs of others. This unhappiness frequently leads to emotional discomfort as the person struggles with emotions of abandonment and unfulfillment.

The exact act of self-sacrifice, which is first done in order to promote connection, ironically causes one's own wellbeing to decline; codependent people may step up their attempts to win over and placate others in reaction to this emotional upheaval, thinking that providing more care will somehow make them feel less alone.

However, the cycle is made worse by this increased emphasis on fulfilling external expectations, as the person gets more involved in the web of co-dependency.

In an attempt to alleviate internal anguish, the co-dependent individual unknowingly perpetuates the pattern by looking for outside approval and trying to influence outside events.

Redirecting the emphasis inside requires conscious effort in order to break the cycle of co-dependency. This entails a significant change in perspective toward appreciating and giving one's own needs, wants, and general wellbeing top priority.

A crucial part of this process is setting healthy, defined boundaries, which help people define their emotional and physical spaces.

Establishing limits in relationships is not a sign of selfishness; rather, it is an essential first step in creating a true connection via mutual respect and understanding.

It becomes clear that self-reflection is an effective strategy for ending the co-dependent cycle. It entails a brave investigation into the causes of co-dependent behaviours, which are frequently derived from traumatic experiences or early life events.

People can start to untangle the emotional baggage that keeps harmful relationship dynamics alive by learning the causes of co-dependency.

This self-awareness act as a guide for those who want to break free from the co-dependent pattern; getting help from trusted friends, therapists, or support groups is essential to ending the co-dependent pattern.

Expert advice provides insightful analysis and useful strategies for navigating the challenges of co-dependency, while social support builds a network of sympathy and encouragement.

Connecting with others who are going through similar things helps to build a feeling of community and reaffirms that overcoming co-dependency is a common and doable objective.

Essentially, ending the cycle of co-dependency is a complex and transforming process that calls for outside assistance, self-reflection, boundary-setting, and self-awareness.

People can free themselves from co-dependency's recurring patterns by deliberately shifting the attention to their own autonomy and well-being.

This path creates the foundation for relationships that are healthier, more harmonious, and based on genuine self- and other-connection as well as respect and understanding.

# CHAPTER 6

# SETTING HEALTHY BOUNDARIES

A vital first step in ending the co-dependent cycle and promoting better relationships is setting appropriate limits. In order to foster emotional stability and independence, this chapter delves into the significance of boundaries, the difficulties in setting them, and doable tactics for doing so.

Boundaries are the mental, physical, and emotional restrictions people place on themselves in order to preserve their sense of self and safeguard their well-being when discussing co-dependency.

Because they are preoccupied with satisfying the demands of others, co-dependents frequently have difficulty setting boundaries because they lose sight of their own autonomy and personal space.

Fear of disagreement or rejection poses a significant obstacle when establishing limits. The fear that voicing their wants may damage their relationships or earn them criticism from others is a common concern among co-dependent people.

Many times, this dread stems from earlier encounters where being oneself could have had unfavourable outcomes.

To get over this anxiety, one must adopt a new viewpoint, acknowledge that respect and understanding are the foundation of healthy relationships, and realize that emotional well-being depends on the establishment of boundaries.

Self-awareness is a crucial element in establishing appropriate limits. To properly communicate wants, desires, and limitations to others, people must first recognize their own.

A candid evaluation of what is individually appropriate and what transcends the bounds of one's physical or emotional well-being is required throughout this process of self-reflection.

In establishing boundaries, communication must be done effectively. To express requirements without seeming aggressive or guilty, one must communicate clearly and assertively.

As they convey wants and feelings without laying responsibility elsewhere, "I" comments can be especially beneficial.

Using the phrase "I need some alone time to recharge" as an example works better than making accusations. Maintaining appropriate limits also requires consistency.

Establishing and enforcing boundaries may cause co-dependent people to run against opposition or backlash. Maintaining these limits requires unwavering resolve in order to underscore the importance of prioritizing one's own well-being.

Reliability fosters confidence and conveys that the limits established are immutable. It's critical to distinguish between flexible and inflexible borders. Well-defined limits are adaptable, facilitating personal development and relationship modifications over time.

Conversely, closeness and intimacy might be hampered by inflexible limits. Recognizing the value of preserving one's independence while continuing to be receptive to sincere connection and vulnerability is necessary to strike the correct balance; boundary-setting requires self-compassion practice, too.

Fearing they are being harsh or selfish, co-dependents may struggle with emotions of guilt or worry while setting boundaries. Knowing that establishing boundaries is not a rejection of other people but rather an act of self-love and self-care is crucial.

People can prioritize their well-being without giving in to guilt by adopting a self-compassionate attitude. Boundary setting can be made more successful by using mindfulness practices.

Through practicing mindfulness, people can better comprehend their needs and emotions by learning to live in the present moment. With more clarity and focus in their relationship management, people can set boundaries according to their emotional state and establish boundaries.

Setting appropriate limits is a transforming process that calls for self-compassion, constancy, self-awareness, and good communication.

People may create boundaries that support emotional health, encourage independence, and help to create healthier, more balanced relationships by getting over their fear of rejection, realizing the value of open communication, and engaging in self-compassion practices.

# CHAPTER 7

# FOCUSING ON SELF-CARE

In order to overcome co-dependency and promote a happier, more balanced existence, self-care is an essential component of the process.

We'll discuss the importance of self-care, how it helps break co-dependent behaviours, and useful tactics for developing a self-care regimen that lasts and builds resilience and emotional health.

Self-care extends beyond superficial pursuits and is sometimes misinterpreted as simple indulgence or pampering. It is an insightful and deliberate practice to tend to one's bodily, mental, and emotional needs.

Those who are deeply committed to co-dependency may find the idea of self-care alien, as their default setting is usually to take care of others. Breaking the cycle of co-dependency requires understanding and embracing self-care. This is a transforming step.

Realizing how important it is to put one's own needs first, guilt-free and without reservation, is a crucial component of self-care.

This change in perspective may initially be difficult for co-dependent people who are used to putting the needs of others before their own.

But it's critical to realize that taking care of oneself is not selfish—rather, it's a necessary condition for total wellbeing.

It entails admitting that people are better able to make constructive contributions to their relationships and the community when they take care of themselves.

The first step in creating a self-care regimen is self-awareness.

Determining one's own requirements and goals is they related to mental clarity, emotional stability, or physical health, is the first step towards creating a customized self-care strategy.

This could entail doing a variety of things, such working out frequently, getting enough sleep, taking up hobbies, or getting counselling. Adapting the schedule to each person's needs and preferences is crucial.

It takes effort to commit time for self-care activities when incorporating them into daily life. People may need to get over their guilt or opposition to taking time for themselves, and time management becomes an essential ability.

It is crucial to understand that self-care builds emotional resilience and the capacity to overcome obstacles, making it an investment in long-term well-being.

Physical, emotional, and mental well-being are all included in a holistic self-care regimen. Physical self-care is taking care of one's body through regular exercise, a healthy diet, and enough sleep.

Spending time with loved ones, journaling, and practicing mindfulness are examples of emotional self-care techniques that centre on fostering happy emotions.

Mentally stimulating hobbies and pastimes like reading, picking up new abilities, or creating art are examples of mental self-care. Effective self-care is based on self-compassion.

Because they are used to putting other people before themselves, co-dependents may feel guilty or resistant to making time for themselves.

Acquiring self-compassion entails realizing that taking care of oneself is an essential rather than an indulgence.

It is a self-loving deed that restores the inner reserves required to maintain wholesome relationships and face life's obstacles. Setting limits in relationships is another aspect of self-care that goes beyond individual activities.

Establishing limits about personal time and communicating one's need for self-care can help foster relationships that are healthier and more kind.

Setting limits and practicing self-care go hand in hand, reinforcing the idea that one's own wellbeing is a non-negotiable.

One of the most important things in overcoming co-dependency is putting self-care first.

It entails a mentality change—realizing how crucial it is to put one's own wants and wellbeing first, guilt-free.

Building emotional resilience and promoting a more balanced existence are two benefits of creating a customized self-care regimen that includes physical, emotional, and mental well-being practices.

Self-care is a crucial step toward escaping co-dependent tendencies and adopting a happier, healthier lifestyle. It is also an investment in one's own personal development.

# CHAPTER 8

# PRIORITIZING YOUR NEEDS

Setting one's needs first is a crucial step in the healing process that separates co-dependency from oneself.

This chapter will discuss the importance of prioritizing one's own needs, the difficulties that come with making this change, and doable tactics for cultivating a perspective that supports one's own well-being while maintaining connections.

People who are co-dependent frequently put other people's needs ahead of their own.

Because personal needs are subordinated to the wants and expectations of others, this repetitive pattern can lead to a distorted sense of self-worth and well-being.

One of the most important steps in escaping the co-dependent cycle is realizing how important it is to prioritize one's needs.

Comprehending the causes of co-dependency is essential to appreciating the difficulties involved in placing one's own needs first.

Frequently stemming from early life encounters or previous traumas, co-dependency presents as an acquired conduct in which people get their feeling of worth from outside sources.

It takes deliberate effort to reframe one's self-worth based on internal validation rather than external approval in order to break out from this deeply ingrained cycle.

Overcoming guilt or selfishness is a big obstacle when it comes to putting one's needs first.

Redirecting attention towards themselves might cause co-dependents, which are used to putting others before themselves, to feel guilty.

It is critical to understand that putting one's needs first is not selfish but rather a necessary component of emotional health and self-care.

People might create a more positive mentality by admitting and dealing with their guilt.

Setting personal needs first is a journey that requires effective communication. Effectively communicating one's needs, wants, and boundaries in a relationship is a skill that upholds the value of personal wellbeing.

This entails being aggressive in expressing demands, speaking in a courteous and straightforward manner, and encouraging candid communication with others.

Positive relationship dynamics are created when there is effective communication, which lays the groundwork for mutual understanding and cooperation.

Setting one's needs first is a process that is simultaneous to developing self-esteem. Because co-dependent people get their feeling of worth from outside approval, co-dependency frequently results in lower self-esteem.

A healthy sense of self-worth can be developed via participating in activities that support a positive self-image, creating and completing personal goals, and recognizing one's skills.

People who have higher self-esteem are better at putting their needs first without being burdened by self-doubt.

In partnerships, putting one's needs first is essential to setting limits. Boundaries define what is appropriate and what goes too far to establish a foundation for constructive interaction.

Establishing and successfully communicating these limits creates an atmosphere in which people value and take into account each person's unique requirements.

Setting priorities for personal needs begins with developing a self-empowerment mindset.

Acknowledging the agency and power that people possess over their own lives is necessary for this.

Proactive decision-making, accepting accountability for one's actions, and negotiating interpersonal interactions with a feeling of independence are all encouraged by empowerment.

Resilience is fostered by a self-empowered perspective, which empowers people to confidently prioritize their needs.

Setting personal needs first is a transforming process that calls for mental clarity, effective communication, and self-awareness.

A better relationship with oneself and others can be developed through letting go of guilt, increasing self-worth, establishing boundaries, and developing a sense of empowerment.

It is crucial that those who want to escape co-dependent behaviours are inspired to adopt a perspective that prioritizes their own needs, which will ultimately lead to a more contented and balanced existence.

# CHAPTER 9

# FINDING BALANCE IN YOUR RELATIONSHIPS

Attaining balance in relationships is essential to freeing oneself from co-dependency and cultivating connections that are not only more robust but also healthier.

Next, we'll talk about the importance of equilibrium, the challenges that come with achieving it, and practical strategies for creating stability in the context of relationships.

When needs and wants of one person are prioritized over those of the other, it is common for co-dependency to show up in relationships as an imbalance.

When a mutually beneficial relationship is established, where each person's uniqueness and well-being are equally recognized, balance is achieved. To begin breaking co-dependent habits, one must first understand the importance of balance.

The deeply ingrained tendency of putting other people's needs before of one's own is a major obstacle to reaching balance.

Fearing that doing so will upset the balance in the relationship, co-dependents may find it difficult to express their needs.

Changing one's viewpoint and realizing that balance is crucial for the well-being and sustainability of relationships rather than being the same as selfishness is necessary to overcome this obstacle.

Maintaining balance in relationships requires effective communication at its core.

Communicating needs, wants, and concerns in an open and honest manner promotes understanding between people.

Discussions regarding expectations, boundaries, and personal objectives should all be part of this communication.

People establish a respectful and well-balanced relationship dynamic by fostering an environment that is conducive to open communication.

Boundaries must be established and upheld in order to attain balance. By defining appropriate conduct and valuing individual space, boundaries provide the structure for constructive communication.

Lack of boundaries occurs frequently in co-dependent patterns, which can cause imbalance and entanglement. Assuring that each person's autonomy is respected and recognized requires setting and communicating boundaries.

Another essential component of achieving relationship balance is developing empathy. Emotions and viewpoints of others must be recognized and understood in order to be empathetic.

People who are co-dependent and used to putting other people's demands before of their own may need to practice empathy by listening intently, taking into account opposing views, and recognizing the emotional needs of other partners.

An atmosphere where equilibrium can flourish is fostered by this reciprocal empathy. Finding balance is facilitated by acknowledging and applauding each person's unique talents and accomplishments.

Shrugging off one's own achievements so as not to take attention away from others is a common feature of co-dependent tendencies.

It fosters equality and mutual respect to accept and recognize each person for their distinct abilities and accomplishments.

Celebrating personal successes helps to create a relationship environment that is supportive and encouraging. Achieving equilibrium requires striking a balance between reciprocity and decision-making.

One-sided decisions that favour one person's preferences and desires over another may occur in co-dependent relationships. People must actively include one another in decision-making if they are to break free from this habit.

Both parties will feel appreciated and have a voice in the future of the relationship thanks to this cooperative approach. Balance in the partnership is improved by fostering a sense of autonomy.

The thought of pursuing personal objectives or partaking in activities alone may initially be difficult for co-dependents.

To preserve individuality and make a positive contribution to the partnership from a point of personal fulfillment, however, requires encouraging independence in each partner.

It is possible for both people to develop and flourish independently when they support and encourage one another's endeavours outside of the partnership.

Effective communication, establishing limits, developing empathy, recognizing each person's unique qualities, and promoting independence are all essential to achieving relationship balance.

This is another resource for those who want to escape co-dependent tendencies and build partnerships that are balanced, respectful, and reciprocal.

Accepting these ideas can help people build stronger, longer-lasting relationships that, when placed in the context of a balanced partnership, support personal development and fulfillment.

# CHAPTER 10

# RECOGNIZING YOUR WORTH

Welcome to a chapter dedicated to taking an introspective journey to discover and honour your true self.

Imagine yourself standing in front of a mirror, not so much to correct your appearance as to see yourself honestly – to see your importance, your individuality, and the enormous contribution you make to both your life and the lives of people around you.

Consider a moment when you received a gift that was exquisitely decorated and packaged.

Now picture yourself as that gift. The labels, comments, judgments, and expectations from society make up the wrapping paper.

It's time to open that present and carefully peel away the layers that don't describe who you are in order to see the genuine, priceless essence inside. Realizing your value is like finding a precious jewel inside of yourself.

It's about realizing that your value is independent of other people's perceptions of you or external validation.

Imagine that you are a priceless work of art just by virtue of who you are, rather than what you accomplish for other people.

Let's go on a contemplative expedition. Consider the aspects that make you special, such as your abilities, eccentricities, and areas of personal fulfillment.

Consider these attributes as the various colours on the canvas that is your life.

Acknowledging your value entails taking a step back and admiring the work of art that is only yours. Now think about the stories you've heard about yourself all of your life.

These stories are like the chapters in a book; some are written by you, and some are written by other people when you're feeling down about yourself. It is time to reconsider these stories.

What if you could change the story so that you are portrayed as the strong hero who embraces change and overcomes obstacles? Consider yourself to be a brilliant light within.

It's about letting that light shine brightly, illuminating the way to self-discovery and fulfillment, rather than turning it down to make other people feel comfortable.

Letting rid of the fear of being better than others and accepting your natural genius are necessary steps towards realizing your worth.

Think about the relationships you have in your life: romantic, familial, and friend relationships.

Imagine now that these interactions are a garden in which every individual is a different flower.

How much you nurture others or how vividly their petals bloom does not define your value. It's about taking care of your own garden and letting your own nature blossom when and how it pleases.

Consider self-compassion as a healing salve for the scars you've accrued along the way.

Treating yourself with the same compassion and consideration that you show to others is a necessary part of realizing your own worth.

It's about accepting your flaws, picking up from your errors, and realizing that you are a work in progress that is always changing and developing. Think of the puzzle metaphor.

Your value is comparable to a piece that flawlessly fits into a complex life mosaic. Every component adds to the overall picture's beauty and completion, making it indispensable.

Acknowledging your uniqueness and irreplaceability as well as your importance as a piece of the puzzle is a necessary step towards realizing your worth.

Let's now discuss boundaries. Think of boundaries as the barriers that safeguard your value. These barriers are designed to protect the priceless items inside of you, not to isolate you.

Creating a space where your essence may bloom requires communicating and maintaining boundaries that protect your physical and emotional well-being.

This is what it means to recognize your worth. It's critical to realize that discovering your value is a constant journey rather than a destination as we traverse this path.

It's about asserting your worth, taking time to periodically check in with yourself, and enjoying the complex fabric that is who you are.

Think of this trip as a never-ending adventure where, with every step, every encounter, and every self-reflection time, you rediscover your worth. You are in the spotlight; are you prepared to accept and value your special contribution?

Let's now highlight each person's accomplishments and strengths. Imagine a stage where each couple showcases their individuality and takes a time being in the spotlight.

A balanced relationship celebrates accomplishments rather than downplaying them in order to keep things in balance. This joy turns into a source of empowerment for both parties, solidifying the basis of the bond.

Making decisions turns into a cooperative work of art. It's a duet in which both partners provide notes, rather than a single performance.

Together, you may make decisions that are rich in mutual viewpoints and contribute to a more harmonious melody in your relationship's symphony. It's about writing the story of your trip together.

Within a partnership, independence is an extension rather than a departure. Imagine two trees growing next to each other, each able to reach the sky on its own despite their roots entwining.

Encouraging independence is like giving tree sunlight so they can grow in their own special ways. On this journey, partners uphold each other's uniqueness while encouraging the other's personal development.

Understanding that relationships are an ongoing dance rather than a one-time event is crucial as we explore the idea of balance in them.

It's about finding grace in the lows, enjoying the highs, and adjusting to the shifting rhythm.

So let's walk the tightrope together, not afraid, but excited about co-creating a relationship that represents equality, harmony, and joyous sharing. You're in the spotlight; are you prepared for the next step?

# CHAPTER 11

# FINDING THE RIGHT BALANCE BETWEEN SELF-CARE AND CARE FOR OTHERS

Yes, we are currently in the delicate dance of taking care of ourselves and others.

It's an active act, akin to balancing between tending to your own wellbeing and lending a supportive hand to those in your immediate vicinity on a tightrope.

Let's explore the art of balance and the harmonious relationship between taking care of oneself and others in this fascinating chapter.

Think of yourself as a tightrope walker who must balance not just your own demands but also the wants and welfare of people who are important to you.

Between the pillars of self-nurturing and generosity, there is a tightrope that requires careful balance at every step.

Consider the thrill of learning the balance and performing this high-wire act—a graceful dance in which you and others are embraced. Imagine the idea of equilibrium as a seesaw in an amusement park.

One extreme is self-care, which is the vital task of preserving your own physical, mental, and emotional well-being.

Conversely, there is care for others, which is the act of accompanying and encouraging someone on their path.

Adjusting the weights is necessary to get the ideal balance, making sure that neither end is grounded for an extended period of time. Think of self-care as your aircraft's oxygen mask.

It is recommended that you fasten your mask in the event of turbulence before helping others. Why?

This is due to the fact that when you're depleted, it's impossible to be a source of strength and encouragement.

It's not about putting people last; it's about realizing that taking care of yourself first improves your ability to take better care of others.

Let's now examine the idea of caring for others. Think of it like a ripple in a pond: the things you do have an impact on the lives of others nearby. It's the satisfaction that comes from making a positive difference in someone else's life and enhancing their well-being.

Giving to others is a reciprocal dance that feeds both the giver and the receiver; it's not only an outward act of kindness.

Consider self-care as your own personal garden—a verdant, rich area where you can tend to your own development.

It entails taking care of your emotional landscape, nourishing the seeds of your interests, and soaking in the sun of self-actualization.

This blossoming garden becomes your wellspring of vitality, providing what you need to take care of others and keep it full and sustaining.

Think of your compassion for other people as the strands that make up a tapestry, including interactions and connections into your life.

It's the richness that results from being linked, the beauty of shared moments, and the power of group support.

Taking care of others is not a hardship; rather, it's like playing a part in a collaborative symphony where every note adds to the overall harmony. Let's think about the seesaw once more now.

Consider it a tool that is responsive and flexible rather than hard equipment. The ability to adapt and judge what's needed at any given time is a skill in the art of achieving equilibrium.

There will be instances in which taking care of oneself is more important than taking care of others. It's a dynamic balance, a continuous dance in which adaptability is essential.

Consider your own and other people's well-being as a bird's wings. Together, they enable you to reach new heights. When one wing is neglected, the voyage becomes unbalanced.

It's about using both of their strengths, seeing that self-care and empathy for others work together to help you soar through life. Think of balance as a tightrope that is held between oneself and other people.

It's a continuous negotiation and dance that adjusts to the ever-changing rhythm of life rather than a risky act of favouring one side over the other.

The skill of being present is essential to striking the correct balance, for both you and the people who come and go from your life's fabric.

Let's celebrate the dynamic flow of this dance as we negotiate the fascinating terrain of striking a balance between our own needs and those of others.

It's a colourful seesaw that invites you to experiment with balance rather than a tightrope to be walked with fear.

You embody the art of balance with every movement and adjustment, creating a symphony where you and others harmonize in the lovely song of life.

All eyes are on you. Are you prepared to take the stage for this enthralling dance?

It all comes down to! Now make it matter!

# CHAPTER 12

# COMMUNICATING YOUR NEEDS

Greetings from the lively realm of conversation; where personal connections are shaped by verbal exchanges. See yourself and your wants as performers on a stage and this chapter as a platform where you can come to life.

As you prepare to enter the realm of successful communication, you will find that your goals, boundaries, and wishes are not just communicated but also understood.

Consider the exchange of words, gestures, and emotions in communication as a rhythmic dance. Like dance moves, your demands are necessary for the conversation to flow smoothly from one to the next.

As the choreographer, visualize yourself arranging the steps to portray the nuanced details of your inner world. Making connections to create a symphony is the essence of communication, not just speaking.

Think of the notes of a tune as your requirements. The harmony of the overall composition is enhanced when each note is performed clearly.

To ensure that your needs are truly heard, it is important to communicate effectively by presenting these notes without distortion.

Imagine going through this as a group singing together, with your voice becoming a smooth part of the overall composition. This brings us to our next topic:

**Active listening**: Think of it as a collaborative dance in which both participants are totally involved and present. Understanding the beat and melody that lie beneath the words is just as important as hearing them.

In order to establish a relationship that goes beyond words, active listening makes room for your needs to be recognized. Consider communication as a way to build a bridge that connects your inner world to the outside world.

The foundation of this bridge is you and your needs; they are what keep it strong and stable.

A strong foundation that for mutual understanding to occur between you and other people is established through clearly stating your demands in communication; imagine the path to mutual understanding as this bridge.

As the beating heart of communication, think of assertiveness. The idea is to discover the rhythm that enables you to properly and firmly communicate your demands, not to dominate or be subjugated.

Establishing limits, stating your opinions clearly, and valuing yourself are all components of assertive communication. Imagine your communication moving forward because of this aggressiveness as the constant heartbeat.

Consider the idea of nonverbal communication for a moment. Consider it the dance that your spoken words and your gestures, facial expressions, and body language make together.

The nuances of your non-verbal cues also communicate your requirements, which are not limited to verbal representation alone. Think of this dancing as a subdued yet effective addition to the dialogue.

Think of empathy as the ability to see other people's dance. It involves placing yourself in their position, sensing the beat of their emotions, and recognizing their requirements.

Building an environment where your needs and others' needs are acknowledged and respected is a key component of empathetic communication.

Consider this empathy to be the synchronicity that turns a conversation into a shared experience.

It is now time to discuss the idea of useful criticism. See it like an interactive conversation in which you may communicate your wants and get helpful feedback in return.

Feedback is the process of starting a dialogue in which you speak up and your comments help to improve understanding over time.

Visualize this feedback loop as an ongoing, dynamic dialogue that gets deeper with time.

Imagine a kaleidoscope of viewpoints while thinking about communication. The framework of shared experiences and differing perspectives encompasses your demands, which are not discrete.

In order to create a mosaic where each viewpoint adds to the richness of the debate, effective communication requires respecting this diversity.

Consider the threads of respect and understanding that weave this kaleidoscope like a tapestry.

Imagine it as an interactive dance, a song, a heart-to-heart bridge, or a rainbow of common viewpoints as we enter the dynamic realm of communicating your wants.

This chapter is not merely a static work; rather, it is a dynamic investigation into understanding and connection.

The attention is on you! Simply walk onto the stage and let your voice to be heard in the harmonious composition of successful communication.

# CHAPTER 13

# DEALING WITH RESISTANCE

The fascinating terrain of resistance navigation is one in which obstacles serve as chances for development rather than as barriers.

Imagine this as an exciting journey in which you put on your explorer's hat and go out to discover the subtleties of resistance in the dynamics of your relationships as well as within yourself.

Prepare yourself for a voyage filled with flexibility, resilience, and revolutionary change.

Consider resistance to be a strong chess opponent. The strategic component that gives the contest complexity and intensity should be avoided, not the opponent.

Similar to the pieces on the board, your movements are deliberate techniques to negotiate and comprehend the resistance rather than only reflexive reactions.

Consider this checkerboard to be the canvas of your relationships, with every move having the capacity to bring about change. Think of resistance like what you might find in a weightlifting exercise.

It's a necessary challenge that fortifies resilience and fortitude rather than something to be feared.

Lifting, pushing, and overcoming obstacles in relationships is similar to the process of growing muscle in weightlifting.

Imagine this strength as the resilience that enables you to overcome obstacles. Let's now examine the idea of active listening in relation to resistance.

Think of it as a dialogue, a discussion in which resistance is greeted with an open mind rather than defensiveness.

When facing resistance, active listening is delving into the subtleties that lie beneath the surface and making an effort to understand the unspoken layers that add to the difficulty.

Imagine that the secrets concealed inside resistance may be unlocked with the help of this active listening. Consider empathy as the salve that heals the scars left by resistance.

Acknowledging and recognizing the feelings underlying the resistance is more important than agreeing. An understanding based on empathy builds a bridge, a link that gets across obstacles.

Imagine this empathy as the healing balm that promotes comprehension and opens the door to cooperative solutions. Think of resilience as the ability to overcome obstacles and turn them into an advantage.

It's important to accept obstacles as necessary for personal development rather than trying to avoid them.

Resilience is the ability to adjust to the curves that resistance throws at you and come out stronger and more skilled at negotiating the intricacies of relationships.

Imagine this resilience as the dynamic force that drives you ahead, turning opposition into a spark that ignites change for the better.

Let's now picture self-awareness as the map that leads you across the resistance-filled area.

Think of it as a tool to better understand your personal triggers and responses to obstacles.

Being self-aware entails, being able to identify moments of resistance within you and respond to them with authenticity and intention. Imagine this self-awareness as the guidance that comes from the North Star when faced with obstacles.

Think of good communication as the means of bridging the difficult waters of resistance. It's more important to pave the road for mutual understanding and cooperation than it is to push your way through.

Clarity in expressing your needs and opinions is essential to creating a conversation that breaks down barriers to communication.

Imagine this communication as the link between you and other people, allowing you to travel through the difficulties together.

Consider compromise as the skill of striking a middle ground in the face of opposition. Finding solutions that respect the needs of everyone concerned is more important than giving up on your demands.

In the face of opposition, compromise entails realizing our shared humanity and identifying the connecting threads that together create an understanding mosaic.

Imagine this compromise as the harmonious combination that turns conflict into unity.

Imagine resistance as a spark for change rather than as a barrier as we enter the dynamic realm of overcoming it. It's not a fight to be won or lost, but rather a chance to learn, a chance to strengthen bonds, a call to develop resilience.

Imagine this trip as an exploration of unexplored ground, where each turn serves as a stepping stone for deeper relationships and self-discovery.

# CHAPTER 14

# MOVING FORWARD

Greetings from the dynamic world of forward motion, where the past and present collide and your actions now determine the course of your future.

Imagine this chapter as an exciting voyage, an exploration into uncharted territory for personal development and metamorphosis.

Prepare to throw off the moorings of the past and venture out into the vast expanse of opportunities, where every decision serves as a compass directing your path ahead.

Consider the idea of flowing forward like a strong river. It's more important to navigate the current skilfully than to fight against it.

You must ride the waves of change and let time's river carry you to new places on your trip.

Imagine this river as the power that moves you ahead, a place where the waters of resilience and adaptability blend with the currents of growth and evolution.

Think of introspection as the compass that directs your boat along the river of progress. It's important to learn from past mistakes rather than focusing on them.

Reflecting on oneself entails taking a critical look at the past, drawing lessons from it, and making decisions that are in line with your changing identity.

Imagine this compass as the instrument that enables you to successfully traverse the waves of personal development.

Let's now examine the idea of forgiveness as the wind that lifts your sails as you proceed on. Think of forgiveness as letting go of the heavy loads that bind you, rather than as approving of the past.

Acknowledging the hurt, giving yourself permission to let go, and letting the compassionate breezes carry you ahead are all part of the forgiveness process.

Imagine this wind as the power that pushes your sails forward, bringing your ship closer to the dawn of fresh opportunities.

Consider thankfulness as the rudder that guides your vessel across the river of progress. It's important to acknowledge the blessings amid the turbulence rather than dismiss obstacles.

Experiencing gratitude entails valuing the knowledge acquired, the advantages acquired, and the development facilitated by the experience.

Imagine this rudder as your vessel's stabilizing instrument, directing you with an awareness of the here and now.

Think of goal-setting as the road plan that shows you where to travel in order to go ahead. The key is to develop intentions that are consistent with your values and goals rather than following strict plans.

Establishing goals entails mapping out the end point, dividing the voyage into doable segments, and making your way toward the shores of your dreams.

See this map as the guide that leads you down the river, making sure that every stroke of the paddle brings you one step closer to the future you want.

Let's now see resilience as the life jacket that helps you stay afloat on the going forward river. Think of resilience as rising above obstacles rather than running away from them.

Accepting setbacks as a necessary part of the path, growing from them, and emerging stronger and more flexible are all components of resilience.

Imagine this life jacket as the buoyant energy that keeps you aloft in spite of the water's turmoil.

Think of curiosity as the compass that points you in the direction of the beautiful sights along the river of progress.

It's important to appreciate the beauty around every corner rather than becoming fixated on the final destination.

Being curious entails keeping an open mind to new things, trying to comprehend the variety of environments, and taking pleasure in the adventure as it unfolds.

Think of this compass as your tour guide, inspiring you to discover and enjoy every second of the journey.

Consider cooperation as the group that travels with you on the ship of progress. It's about making relationships and sharing the experience, not about navigating alone.

Building connections of support, taking advice from others, and forging ahead as a group are all part of collaboration.

Imagine this group as your traveling companions who add flavour and significance to the experience.

Imagine the dynamic river of going forward as a network of interrelated currents, bends, and coasts rather than a straight line as we traverse it.

Instead of being a race, it's an ongoing discovery and adventure where the trip is just as important as the final destination. Imagine every moment as a ripple in the river that adds to your life's ever-changing scenery.

# CHAPTER 15

# LIVING A FULFILLING LIFE

This is a colourful picture of leading a happy life, where each stroke of the brush adds to the masterpiece that is your life.

Consider this chapter as a gallery of opportunities, a call to fully engage with the hues, patterns, and feelings that mould a life full of significance and meaning.

Prepare to discover the essence of fulfillment, where every decision turns into an artistic brushstroke that illustrates your singularly fulfilling journey.

Think of leading a happy life as a magnificent symphony. It's more important to recognize the tasteful interaction of many components than it is to achieve a crescendo.

The melody of your passions, the rhythm of relationships, and the crescendos of personal development make up the symphony of your life.

Imagine this symphony as the music that plays throughout your life, urging you to dance to the sounds of sincerity and happiness.

Think of passion as the spark in your life's tapestry that ignites the flames of fulfillment. It's more important to cultivate a range of passions that brighten your days than it is to locate one solitary glowing ember.

Pursuing pursuits that fulfill your spirit entails bringing excitement and a feeling of purpose to every moment. Think of these passions as the vivid colours that accentuate the details and depth on your life's canvas.

Let's now examine the idea of purpose as the compass that guides you on your path to living a happy and meaningful life.

Consider your purpose as the driving force that ensures your activities are consistent with your goals and beliefs rather than as a destination.

Asking important questions, looking for meaningful answers, and negotiating the complex paths that lead to a meaningful existence are all part of finding one's purpose.

Imagine this compass as the tool that guides you through the vast ocean of opportunity. Consider thankfulness as the multicoloured kaleidoscope that reflects the light of fulfillment.

It's important to see the abundance all around you rather than ignoring difficulties.

Experiencing gratitude is realizing the little victories, the deep relationships, and the basic pleasures that turn every day into a work of art.

See the beauty and richness of your life through the lens of this kaleidoscope. Think of resilience as the rock that keeps you afloat in the constantly shifting waves of a meaningful existence.

It's more important to withstand storms with grace and power than to avoid them.

Being resilient entails accepting failures as chances for personal development, rising above obstacles, and emerging from hardships with fresh perspective.

Imagine this anchor as the steadying influence that gives you the courage to confidently traverse the erratic currents.

So let us see growth as the flower that is about to bloom in the garden of living a meaningful life.

Consider growth as the ongoing realization of your potential rather than a straight line. To grow is to accept new experiences, grow from setbacks, and become the best version of oneself.

Consider this flower as a representation of rebirth and metamorphosis, blooming in reaction to the sustenance provided by life's diverse experiences.

Consider connection to be the threads that, when combined, create a tapestry of relationships on the canvas of a happy life.

The kinds of relationships that enhance your trip are more important than the number of them.

Establishing connections, feeling a part of something, and creating a network of people who support you all contribute to a better experience.

Imagine these threads as the complex patterns that weave together moments of love, support, and shared experiences to form a tapestry.

Think of mindfulness as the prism through which the specifics of leading a happy life become clear. Savouring the current moment is more important than thinking about the past or the future.

To practice mindfulness, you must immerse yourself in the beauty of the present moment, appreciate the textures of experience, and be totally present.

Consider this lens as the instrument that enables you to recognize, experience, and appreciate the fullness of every passing moment.

As we explore the fascinating world of leading a happy life, try to picture it as a journey rather than a final destination—a work of art that changes and grows every day.

It involves actively contributing to the building of a life that aligns with your core values and aspirations rather than passively waiting for fulfillment to come knocking on your door.

Imagine that you are the journey's artist, composer, and guide, creating a tapestry that depicts the symphony of a genuinely satisfying existence.

# CHAPTER 16

# LETTING GO OF OLD PATTERNS

Welcome to the fascinating world of shedding old skin, a metamorphosis in which the past vanishes and a new self emerges.

See this chapter as a celebration of your ability to transcend and let go of the habits that no longer serve you, like to a phoenix rising from the ashes.

Prepare yourself for an exhilarating trip where letting go turns into a freeing dance toward personal development and metamorphosis. Consider letting go of ingrained behaviours as a spiritual spring cleaning.

It's more important to dust off any cobwebs that may have accumulated over time than it is to reject your past.

You must examine the patterns of your behaviours, attitudes, and routines in order to determine what no longer reflects who you really are.

Imagine this spring cleaning as a breath of fresh air that fills your life with clarity and rejuvenation. Think of self-awareness as the flashlight that reveals the obscure details in your ingrained habits.

It's not about passing judgment, but rather bringing attention to the ingrained habits and reflexive reactions that might have been going unnoticed.

Being self-aware is looking at oneself with interest, peeling back the layers, and discovering the causes of your habits.

Imagine that this flashlight is your guide, enabling you to make your way through the maze that is your subconscious mind. Let us now investigate the idea of compassion as the tender hug that goes along with letting go.

See compassion as holding space for the aspects of you that may have been functioning from a place of fear or conditioning, rather than as giving in to ingrained habits.

Recognizing your humanity, pardoning past transgressions, and cultivating an atmosphere of self-love are all components of compassion.

Imagine this kindness as the warm sunlight that nourishes the fragile new growth buds inside of you.

See mindfulness as the rock that keeps you anchored in the here and now when you're letting go.

It's about grounding yourself in the present moment rather than thinking back on previous transgressions or imagining future difficulties.

A sense of presence is fostered, thoughts and emotions are seen without attachment, and the journey is welcomed with open arms when practicing mindfulness.

Imagine this anchor as the reassuring power that helps you stay balanced while navigating the waves of change.

Think of courage as the spark that starts the letting go process. It's more important to face the uncertainty with bravery and resiliency than it is to avoid discomfort.

To be courageous means to choose progress over stagnation, to face the fears that may come with letting go, and to enter the transformational arena.

Imagine this flame as the lighthouse that illuminates your way and leads you through the unknown regions of self-discovery.

Currently, consider acceptance as the key that opens the door to letting go. Consider acceptance as a deliberate decision to accept the truth of your experiences without opposition, rather than as a sign of surrender.

Acceptance is accepting that past behaviours are temporary, finding contentment in your path, and becoming receptive to the limitless opportunities that lay ahead.

Imagine this key as the means of breaking free from the bonds of attachment to the past.

Resilience can be compared to the music that plays while you let go. It's more important to recover gracefully and powerfully from setbacks than it is to avoid them.

Being resilient entails overcoming obstacles, adjusting to changing conditions, and being wiser as a result of letting go. Imagine this song as the pulse that helps you let go of old habits as you move fluidly.

Think of purpose as the compass that directs your movements throughout the release dance. Instead of aiminglessly cruising, you should chart a path that is consistent with your goals and ideals.

Choosing your path for growth, making a plan for the future, and traveling with purpose are all parts of intentionality. Think of this compass as the tool that helps you match your actions to your changing vision.

Imagine this process of letting go of old patterns as an embracing of your always changing self rather than a break with the past as we negotiate its complicated dance.

It is not about wiping out the past; rather, it is about rewriting the narrative and selecting the stories that inspire and empower. Imagine yourself as the master of your own metamorphosis, the choreographer of this dance, and the builder of this rejuvenation.

# CHAPTER 17

# FORGIVING YOURSELF AND OTHERS

Greetings from the vast terrain of forgiveness, a sacred place where opportunities for healing and liberation are created from the weight of the past;

Imagine this chapter as a haven where learning the skill of forgiveness turns into a transforming journey that affects oneself and others.

Prepare to go into the profound realms of forgiveness—both of yourself and of others—where the alchemy of compassion and release makes room for rebirth.

Consider forgiveness as a link between the coasts of suffering and recovery, suspended above choppy waves.

The goal is to cross the bridge toward understanding, empathy, and, in the end, release rather than to erase the memories of past wounds.

It is up to you to cross this bridge, own the weight of your grievances, and decides which way to go in order to find healing.

Imagine this bridge as the way to overcome emotional constraints and become the builder of healing via forgiveness. Think of self-forgiveness as the soft rain that falls on your soul's garden.

Rather than justifying previous transgressions, it's about extending the self-compassion necessary for personal development.

Understanding the context of your acts, accepting the humanity within you, and letting go of your judgment of yourself are all necessary components of self-forgiveness.

Imagine this rain as the gentle hug that helps you love yourself and makes room for a new you to emerge. Let's now discuss the idea of empathy serving as a compass for you while you forgive others.

Think of empathy as a comprehension of the common human experience rather than as a support for wrongdoing.

Empathy is putting oneself in another person's position, appreciating the complexity of their experience, and realizing the fragility that unites us all.

Imagine this compass as the guide guiding you toward empathy and mutual understanding.

See compassion as the salve that soothes the pain from the past. It's about putting understanding above resentment, not about supporting destructive behaviour.

Having compassion means realizing the suffering you have caused, showing others and yourself empathy, and creating a space where healing can occur.

Imagine this cream as the salve that turns cuts into scars—marks that serve as symbols of tenacity and fortitude.

Think of resilience as the cornerstone that holds the forgiveness edifice in place. Building a future that emerges from the ashes of suffering is more important than erasing the past.

Resilience entails growing the capacity to forgive and move on, learning from mistakes, and recovering from setbacks. See this base as the stable soil where the seeds of forgiveness can grow and bear fruit.

Now, consider the idea of letting go as the key to opening the doors to forgiveness.

Imagine forgiving someone not as a way to avoid taking responsibility, but rather as a deliberate decision to let go of resentment.

Letting go is deciding to walk the path of emotional emancipation, giving up the need for vengeance, and releasing oneself from the bonds of anger.

Imagine this key as the key that unlocks the doors to a more tranquil and complete you.

Consider forgiveness as a fabric made of strands that represent empathy, release, and understanding.

It's important to weave the hurtful strands into a pattern that illustrates development and transformation rather than trying to erase them.

Recognizing the interdependence of all things and the beauty that results from compassion weaved together are necessary components of forgiveness.

Imagine this tapestry as the masterpiece that graces your life's canvas, demonstrating the creative power of forgiveness. Think of intention as the lighthouse illuminating the forgiveness path.

It's important to chart a deliberate path for reconciliation rather than just haphazardly moving forward. To forgive is to consciously choose to do so, to commit to healing, and to express a desire for both parties to be happy.

Imagine this lantern as the lighthouse that provides you with direction and clarity while you navigate the maze of forgiveness.

Imagine forgiveness as a continuous process, a dynamic dance of healing and release, rather than as a single act as we explore the complex terrain of forgiveness.

Instead of eliminating the past, the goal is to use it as a source of compassion and insight. See yourself as the forgiver, the painter who creates a masterpiece of rebirth on a canvas with empathy and understanding.

# CHAPTER 18

# MOVING ON FROM TOXIC RELATIONSHIPS

This is the uplifting path of breaking free from unhealthy relationships that are weighing you down. Come explore the possibilities of coming out of the shadows.

Here, the bonds of toxic relationships are broken and the road to regaining your autonomy is unveiled.

It's a place of strength. Through the maze of poisonous situations, it finds its way out and comes out stronger, more confident, and with a fresh perspective on its own value.

See ending unhealthy relationships as an attempt to find direction in a confusing environment. Eliminating the haze obstructing your eyesight is more important than forsaking people.

It's up to you to identify the qualities of a toxic relationship, admit how it affects your health, and take back the freedom to breathe in the clean air of fulfilling relationships.

Imagine yourself navigating the maze with this clarity acting as your compass.

Think of yourself as protected from toxic relationships by your armour of self-respect. To protect your emotional and mental well-being, set limits rather than erecting walls.

Having self-respect means; having the guts to stick up for yourself when people try to violate your boundaries, realizing your own value, and facing negativity head-on.

Imagine yourself navigating the obstacles with strength and resiliency thanks to this armour, which acts as a protective shield.

Let us now investigate the idea that self-reflection serves as a lantern in toxic relationships, illuminating the shadows.

View introspection as a call to understand your own needs and tendencies rather than as a means of placing blame on you.

Making decisions that are in line with your values, assessing how you fit into the dynamics, and considering your own part in them are all components of self-reflection.

Imagine yourself walking out of the dark with the help of this lantern.

Encouraging relationships can be accessed by using empowerment as the key. Accepting responsibility for your own pleasure is more important than placing blame.

Recognizing your agency to write your own story, acting in accordance with your moral principles, and taking back control of your life are all necessary steps toward empowerment.

See this key as the key that unlocks the door to self-determination and releases you from the bonds of victimization. When it comes to letting go of unhealthy relationships, think of support as the link that connects you to a network of allies.

The goal is to connect with people who support and understand you, not to isolate yourself.

A safety net that promotes your development must be established, advice from dependable friends or experts must be sought, and your experiences must be shared.

Imagine that the path to understanding and connection is this bridge. Now imagine the idea of forgiveness as the healing salve applied to the injuries caused by poisonous relationships.

Consider forgiving someone as relinquishing their grasp on your mental health rather than endorsing bad behaviour.

In order to be forgiven, you must first acknowledge your suffering, then give yourself permission to let go, and then let time cure you.

See this salve as the catalyst for transformation that opens the door to emotional healing.

When you consider resilience, picture it as the strong boat that helps you navigate the rough seas of ending toxic relationships.

The goal is to weather the storms with resilience and fortitude, not to run from difficulties. Learning from failures, overcoming hardship, and coming out on the other side with a renewed sense of self are all parts of being resilient.

Think of this boat as your tool for navigating the waves of transition. After you have moved on from toxic relationships; think of authenticity as the compass that points you in the direction of true connections.

In relationships, it's more important to be authentic than to hide behind facades.

Upholding your principles, being open about your needs, and drawing people who connect with your true self are all components of authenticity.

Think of this compass as your reliable guide toward sincere and respectful relationships. Consider it an ongoing journey towards self-discovery and growth as we navigate the maze of ending toxic relationships.

Entering the present with a fresh sense of agency and purpose is more important than wallowing in the past. Consider yourself as the fearless adventurer, exploring uncharted ground in terms of empowerment and connection.

# CHAPTER 19

# BUILDING A SUPPORT SYSTEM

Here, in the centre of connection, resilience and personal development are rooted in a robust support network.

Welcome to this place!

This is a joint endeavour that delves into the skill of creating a support system that helps you weather the ups and downs of life.

I look forward to learning the value of relying on others and being there for them in return, building a community where strength in unity becomes an unstoppable force.

See the process of creating a support system as similar to that of building a bridge across choppy waters.

Having solid structures and trustworthy connections to assist you overcome obstacles is more important than trying to navigate the currents on your own.

You must seek out people who can serve as your bridge's pillars, acknowledge the qualities they offer, and cultivate relationships that can withstand adversity.

Imagine that the avenue to shared resilience and support is this bridge.

In the architecture of a support system, think of vulnerability as the foundation of true connectivity. Becoming authentically you doesn't indicate weakness; rather, it takes guts.

In order to create a space where others feel safe to reciprocate, vulnerability entails revealing your pleasures, frustrations, and anxieties.

Imagine that this cornerstone serves as the firm foundation that trust is formed upon, fostering the development of real connections.

It is time to investigate the idea of reciprocity as the life force that permeates a support system. Think of reciprocity as a constant flow of compassion and understanding rather than as a transaction.

When you provide assistance when required and gently accept it in return, you are engaging in reciprocity, which fosters a dynamic flow that fortifies the ties around you.

Consider this flow to be the lifeblood that keeps your support network strong.

Consider empathy to be the cement that holds a support system together. Comprehending and acknowledging the feelings of others is more important than offering solutions.

To be empathetic, one must put oneself in another person's shoes, listen without passing judgment, and foster an atmosphere in which each person's experiences are valued. Think of the mortar as the glue that holds the pieces together and creates a sturdy framework that will not crumble over time.

Think of diversity as your support system's mosaic, adding colour and depth. It is more important to embrace a variety of viewpoints and experiences rather than surrounding yourself with exact duplicates.

In order to create a mosaic that portrays the complexity of life, diversity entails appreciating the special talents that each individual provides.

Imagine the artwork that adds to the strength and beauty of your support system—this mosaic.

This time, let's imagine that communication is the language that is spoken inside your support network. Visualize discourse as a continuous process that builds relationships rather than as a monologue.

Active listening, voicing demands, and creating a space where everyone's voice is heard are all components of communication.

Consider this language to be the background music that permeates your network and produces a melodic symphony.

Consider boundaries to be the structure that keeps your support system stable and strong. The goal should be to set boundaries that respect each person's well-being rather than to build barriers.

In order to avoid burnout and promote a long-lasting support system, boundaries entail knowing when to ask for and when to give assistance.

Think of these boundaries as the structural components that provide your network strength and organization.

See trust as the freely flowing cash in your support system's economy. The confidence that grows from constant dependability and comprehension is what matters, not blind faith.

Building an environment where people feel comfortable disclosing their vulnerabilities and maintaining secrecy are all necessary components of trust.

Consider this money as the precious trade that strengthens the ties in your support system.

Imagine this as a team effort rather than a solitary project as we dive into the complex concept of creating a support system.

It is more important to build a tribe that shares your beliefs, is aware of your journey, and is able to persevere through life's setbacks than it is to surround oneself with an army.

Consider yourself the network's architect, creating a framework that promotes common development, strength, and connection.

# CHAPTER 20

# EMBRACING A NEW IDENTITY

Welcome to the culmination of your life-changing adventure – the point at which personal development and self-discovery intertwine to become a whole new self.

It is the apex of something greater than itself, like a phoenix rising from the ashes of the past and into the infinite sky of possibilities.

Prepare yourself for the thrilling journey of letting go of the past and welcoming the present, where your life's canvas is waiting to be painted with the colourful, new identity you choose.

Consider accepting a new identity as if it were the act of going on stage and being the centre of attention.

Becoming the real you that has shown yourself through the many stages of your journey are more important than pretending to be someone you're not.

You are performing for a potential audience and are invited to highlight the depth of your recently discovered identity.

See yourself at this point as the protagonist of your own story, ready to take centre stage and shine with your own authenticity.

When you step onto the stage of a new identity, self-reflection serves as your backstage mirror, allowing you to see yourself clearly.

It's important to acknowledge your development, your strengths, and the lessons that have shaped your evolution rather than criticizing yourself.

In order to lay the groundwork for the authenticity you are going to reveal, self-reflection entails comprehending the nuances of your goals, values, and aspirations.

See this backstage mirror as the instrument that cultivates introspection and creates the atmosphere necessary for a sincere performance.

Let's now examine intention as the plot device that directs the story of your new self.

Instead of viewing intention as a strict script, picture it as a flexible framework that changes as your goals and values do.

Establishing your future self's course, figuring out the persona you wish to represent, and giving your actions meaning are all parts of intention.

Imagine the narrative of your new identity being shaped by this script. Consider bravery as the mask you put on when you decide to adopt a new identity. It's about adorning yourself with the courage to be true to yourself, not about hiding your weaknesses.

It takes courage to push yourself beyond your comfort zone, to embrace uncertainty, and to show the world who you really are.

Consider this costume as the clothing that represents the fortitude and resiliency that come with embracing your new identity.

Think of yourself as the spotlight illuminating your presence on the stage of your new identity— authenticity. Allowing your genuine self to shine is more important than putting on a show.

Standing boldly in the light of your true self, appreciating individuality, and accepting flaws are all components of authenticity.

Envision this spotlight as the radiant radiance that embodies your genuineness, beckoning interaction and resonance.

Let us now visualize the idea of adaptability as the dance moves that enable you to transition smoothly into a new persona.

Consider flexibility as an improvised dance that moves to the beat of life rather than as predetermined steps.

Being adaptable means; knowing how to move through changing circumstances with grace, twisting and turning as your identity changes.

Think of this dance as the dynamic movement that represents your ability to develop and grow.

Consider your gratitude as the thunderous cheers that fill your new identity's auditorium. It's about realizing and celebrating your personal development rather than looking for approval from others.

Relishing the delight of self-discovery, cultivating humility, and appreciating the roles played by the supporting cast in your life's journey are all components of gratitude.

Imagine the affirming sound of this applause echoing the celebration of your transformation.

Think of resilience as your new identity's encore, the performance that comes right after your performance.

It's about overcoming obstacles with newly acquired fortitude and insight rather than trying to avoid them.

Resilience entails overcoming adversity with a refreshed sense of self, learning from experiences, and accepting setbacks with grace.

Think of this encore as your victorious comeback, signifying your capacity to go past setbacks and keep improving.

Imagine that the process of embracing a new identity is a continuous performance rather than a one-time event as you enter the spotlight. It's more important to have a flexible character who can change to fit the way your life unfolds than to have a set role.

Imagine yourself in the roles of protagonist, director, and artist, constantly honing and expressing the masterpiece that is your true self. The scene is set; let your new identity's humorous drama play out.

# CONCLUSION

# A NEW BEGINNING

We are on the verge of a fresh start as we approach the end of this in-depth investigation into the topics of co-dependency healing, creating healthier relationships, and developing a life-changing path toward self-discovery.

The chapters we've read through have been a tapestry with strands of perseverance, self-awareness, and a dedication to growth.

Ours' is a bridge that unites the realizations we have learned along our journey; it invites us to enter the world where the memories of the past act as stepping stones rather than obstacles.

This point in time serves as a doorway for self-reinvention, a blank canvas where opportunity and transformation meet. Handle the complex process of letting go of the past and accepting who you really are.

This change is like a butterfly emerging from its cocoon and spreading its wings to reveal newfound authenticity and freedom.

The path to a new identity involves integrating the lessons learned, revealing layers, and letting your true self come to the surface rather than throwing away the old.

 It entails the practice of self-rediscovery, which is an ongoing investigation of desires, ideals, and goals that could have been obscured by the masks of ingrained habits.

It's an honouring of the individuality that exists within, of the changing self that emerges with every brave stride into unknown lands.

Imagine this procedure as a sculptor removing extraneous details to unveil the work of art that has always been there.

This is how one imagines the dawn emerging from a long night, chasing the darkness and brightening the path ahead.

A fresh start is more than simply a page change; it's a dynamic chapter where the transformational seeds sown along the way come to life as vibrant realities.

Think of this fresh start as a blank canvas ready to be painted with growth, resilience, and intention. It's a call to rethink interpersonal dynamics, establish sensible limits, and steer clear of pitfalls in life with fresh insight.

You now have the tools—forgiveness, creating a network of support, and the ability to let go—to intentionally and authentically design this new beginning, thanks to the chapters that have been covered.

Accept the idea of a fresh start as you venture into this unknown area. View it not as a destination but rather as a constant evolution—a continual dance with life's rhythms.

Every experience you have along the way, no matter how easy or difficult, adds to the work of art you are making. Imagine yourself as the creator, the architect, and the guide of this continuous story, which changes with every breath, decision, and second.

This statement is a declaration that your history does not define you; rather, your ability to change, grows, and learns, gives you power.

It's an admission that the trip continues in this direction and becomes a circular rhythm of ongoing self-revelation and rejuvenation.

Let this ending serve as a call to action as you bid adieu to the chapters that have been covered. You should be ready to start over with excitement, wonder, and a sense of boundless possibilities. The focus is on you—not as an observer but as the main character in this story, prepared to accept the developing tale of your brand-new beginning.